IMAGES
of America

ALLSTON-
BRIGHTON

Newton Street, 1905.

IMAGES
of America

ALLSTON-
BRIGHTON

William Marchione, Ph.D.

ARCADIA

First published 1996
Copyright © William Marchione, Ph.D., 1996

ISBN 0-7524-0487-3

Published by Arcadia Publishing,
an imprint of the Chalford Publishing Corporation
One Washington Center, Dover, New Hampshire 03820
Printed in Great Britain

Library of Congress Cataloging-in-Publication Data applied for

This is Engine Co. #41, somewhere in Allston.

Contents

Acknowledgments

Allston-Brighton was undertaken as a project of the Brighton-Allston Historical Society. All royalties accruing from its publication will go to the support of the society and its activities.

I wish to acknowledge the assistance at every stage in the preparation of this work of the Brighton-Allston Historical Society Publications Committee, consisting of Charlie Vasiliades, Elizabeth Shepard, Aurora Salvucci, and Mary Ann Marchione. The publications committee helped with the acquisition, selection, and arrangement of the photographs appearing in this book; also, it assisted by proofreading the text, and by offering valuable suggestions for alterations. I wish to express particular appreciation to Charlie Vasiliades, current president of the Brighton-Allston Historical Society, for the work he has done over the years to help build up the society's photographic collection.

While we have drawn upon outside collections—especially the Society for the Preservation of New England Antiquities—for some 20 percent of the images appearing herein, the majority of these photographs came from our own collection, which consists of images donated by past and present Allston-Brighton residents. Without these many generous donations of photographs, this work would not have been possible.

Preeminent among donors has been Dr. Roy B. Stewart, one of the founding members of the Brighton-Allston Historical Society. With deep appreciation for the long-term interest the good doctor took in the work of the society, we are pleased to dedicate *Allston-Brighton* to our long-time friend, Dr. Roy B. Stewart.

William P. Marchione, Ph.D.
Curator, Brighton-Allston Historical Society

One
Agricultural Village

The quiet and prosperous agricultural village of Little Cambridge, as Allston-Brighton was originally known, formed a part of the town of Cambridge throughout the colonial era. Its location on the opposite side of the Charles River, then a tidal estuary surrounded by hundreds of acres of salt marshes, at first discouraged settlement. Only in the period from 1647 to 1649, almost two decades after the foundation of the parent town, did three prominent Cambridge families—the Champneys, Sparhawks, and Danas—decide to establish themselves on the river's south side. The Reverend John Eliot's 1646 conversion of the Nonantum Indians to Christianity doubtless encouraged their migration. Other families soon followed. The problems associated with crossing the river were eased somewhat by the construction of the Great Bridge in 1662, at the present-day North Harvard Street crossing.

Little Cambridge enjoyed many natural advantages. Its highly fertile soil and many healthy, elevated, and well-drained farmsteads were very productive. Moreover, the nearby port city of Boston furnished a ready market for the community's produce. The community's location on the Charles River (a natural highway) and on the main road to Boston (the Roxbury and Watertown Highways—today's Harvard Avenue and Washington Street) gave Little Cambridge obvious transportation advantages. By the late 1680s, this small, prospering agricultural village (which then contained a mere two hundred residents) was paying the highest per capita taxes in Cambridge.

During the eighteenth century, a number of prominent men established country estates in Little Cambridge. These included the immensely wealthy Boston merchant Captain Nathaniel Cunningham; James Ward Apthorp, son of the influential war contractor Charles Apthorp; and Benjamin Faneuil, elder brother of Boston merchant and philanthropist Peter Faneuil.

The village of Little Cambridge enjoyed a relatively tranquil relationship with its parent town in the colonial era. The political and religious life of the community was centered in Harvard Square in Cambridge, site of the First Church of Cambridge and of town meetings, but voters at these meetings regularly elected Little Cambridge men as selectmen and often sent them to represent Cambridge in the colony's legislature. In the years just before the Revolution, for example, Thomas Gardner of Little Cambridge was a highly influential political figure.

Only in one respect was there serious friction between the south side community and Cambridge proper. This arose over the thorny issue of ecclesiastical independence. In 1744, Little Cambridge was given permission to establish a local meetinghouse for use in the winter months only, residents having otherwise to travel to the First Church in distant Harvard Square. Also, south side residents were obliged to pay taxes for the support of the Cambridge church. Then, in 1783, after several unsuccessful attempts, the Massachusetts Legislature granted the south side community's petition for a fully independent church, and Little Cambridge took its first major step toward independence.

English settlement on the Charles River began in 1630 with the founding of Watertown and Cambridge. Initially the land comprising Allston-Brighton was assigned to Watertown. In 1634, however, the General Court of the Massachusetts Bay Colony transferred ownership of the "South Side of the River" to Cambridge.

Reverend John Eliot of Roxbury, known to history as the "Apostle to the Indians," made his first conversions on October 18, 1646, in the valley between the Waban and Nonantum Hills on the present Brighton-Newton boundary. In this same valley, the converts established the first Christian Indian community in British North America , calling it Nonantum.

Within the mural, inscribed on a plaque:

JOHN ELIOT PREACHING TO THE INDIANS

I AM ABOUT THE WORK OF THE GREAT GOD
AND MY GOD IS WITH ME

REVEREND JOHN ELIOT

A Memorial Hall mural in the Massachusetts State House, painted by Henry O. Walter in 1903, commemorates John Eliot's Indian conversions. (Commonwealth of Massachusetts, State House Art Collection, courtesy Massachusetts Art Commission, photograph by Douglas Christian.)

The Dana House, built about 1680, stood on Washington Street near the present Allston Street intersection. It was built by a son of Richard Dana, progenitor of the family that produced such notable figures as Congressman Francis Dana and Richard Henry Dana II, author of *Two Years Before the Mast*. Members of the Dana family occupied this dwelling until 1875.

The Brown-Parsons-Duncklee Mansion stood near the present Duncklee/Harriet Street intersection. It was built in the mid-1600s, probably by Thomas Brown. In the early nineteenth century it belonged to Gorham Parsons, a leading horticulturist and experimental farmer. Parsons' Brighton estate was called "Oakland Farms." The last owner, John Duncklee, was a Boston businessman. (Courtesy of the Society for the Preservation of New England Antiquities.)

The Samuel Sparhawk Mansion stood on Western Avenue near the present Antwerp Street intersection and dated from the early 1700s. Sparhawk was a Cambridge selectman from 1737 to 1741. His daughter, Joanna, married Thomas Gardner in 1755. It was to this house that the fatally-wounded Colonel Gardner was carried following the Battle of Bunker Hill in June 1775. The mansion was demolished in 1898.

The Shedd House stood where Atkins Street now intersects Washington Street, just west of Oak Square. Little is known of the history of this mid- to late-seventeenth-century dwelling. In the nineteenth century it was the home of the Charles Shedd family. (Courtesy of the Society for the Preservation of New England Antiquities.)

The Noah Worcester House, which stood at the northwest corner of Washington and Foster Streets, was built in 1688. In 1813, it became the home of Reverend Noah Worcester, New England's leading pacifist and author of *A Solemn Review of the Custom of War*, the first American work of pacifism. He also served as Brighton's first postmaster from 1817 until 1837. (Courtesy of the Society for the Preservation of New England Antiquities.)

The Maccoone-Stratton-Champney House, dating from the late 1600s, was built by Daniel Maccoone, a farmer and shoemaker, and stood on the site of 649 Washington Street, west of Oak Square. In the late 1700s it became the home of Nathaniel Champney. Nathaniel and his son, William Richards Champney, were perennial officeholders in the Brighton of their day.

The identity of the builder of this Faneuil Street house is unknown, but the date over the doorway establishes that it was built in 1707. The Davis House stood on the site of the Faneuil Housing Project. In the early 1800s, the Davis family, butchers by trade, acquired the property. Their slaughterhouse stood to the rear. (Courtesy of the Society for the Preservation of New England Antiquities.)

This eighteenth-century residence, the home of Stutely Burlingame, stood at the intersection of Washington and Beechcroft Streets. A portion of McMurtry's Ledge, a local stone quarry, is visible in the photograph. Part of the wall in the photograph still stands. (Courtesy of the Society for the Preservation of New England Antiquities.)

The Ebenezer Smith House at 15-17 Peaceable Street was built about 1725 and is the oldest house in the Brighton Center area. The Winships, founders of the local cattle industry, lived here in the late 1770s. It was the birthplace of Captain Jonathan Winship, China trade merchant and founder of the local horticultural industry. (Illustration by Richard Salvucci.)

The Baker-Waugh House was built by John Baker, a farmer, in 1709. It stood near the Chestnut Hill Avenue/South Street intersection. Daniel Waugh acquired the farm in 1833, and in 1866 sold part of it to the City of Boston for the construction of the Chestnut Hill Reservoir. (Courtesy of the Society for the Preservation of New England Antiquities.)

This eighteenth-century dwelling stood on the north side of Washington Street in Brighton Center, on the site of 347 Washington Street. A slaughterhouse was situated to its rear in the early 1800s. Jesse Osborn, who owned the house from 1820 into the late 1860s, was a Brighton wheelwright. His wheel-making shop stood a short distance west of the house.

The Little Cambridge Meetinghouse, dating from 1744, was situated at the northeast corner of Washington and Market Streets in Brighton Center. The meetinghouse was at first merely an annex or chapel of the First Church of Cambridge in Harvard Square, intended for use only in winter. It gained religious autonomy in 1783 as the Third Parish Church of Cambridge. Its first permanent minister was the Reverend John Foster. It was in the church parsonage, which still stands at 10 Academy Hill Road, that Reverend Foster's wife, Hannah Webster Foster, wrote her highly successful novel, *The Coquette*, or *The History of Eliza Wharton*, published in 1797.

Much of Allston-Brighton's historic fabric has disappeared, but the Market Street Burying Ground (1764) has stood steadfast against the ravages of time. Before 1764, Little Cambridge residents were laid to rest across the river in Cambridge. Populated by fewer than one hundred gravestones, the Market Street Burying Ground provides a three-dimensional index of the community's early socio-economic development. (Photograph by Annmarie Rowlands.)

While a major portion of the Market Street Burying Ground was obliterated in 1870 when Market Street was widened, the graveyard still contains a representative collection of eighteenth- and nineteenth-century gravestone motifs. The "winged cherub" and "willow and urn" designs predominate. Many of the stones were carved by Newton craftsman Daniel Hastings. (Photograph by Annmarie Rowlands.)

17

In 1760 Benjamin Faneuil, elder brother of Peter Faneuil, bought 70 acres of land on Bigelow Hill, near the present Crittenton-Hastings House, and established the estate pictured here. Reportedly no expense was spared. General Washington and General Arthur Lee dined at the Faneuil Mansion while the Continental Army was headquartered in Cambridge. Later owners included John Parkman (of the prominent Boston Parkman family), who employed as his coachman Harvey D. Parker, founder of the Parker House. In 1839, Samuel Bigelow, prosperous cattle dealer, acquired the estate. The Bigelows occupied it into the present century. The mansion was destroyed by fire in 1919, but the estate's foundations still exist in the Crittenton Woods urban wild. The roads visible in the photograph are Washington Street (foreground) and Faneuil Street.

This heraldic crest is found on the Faneuil tomb in the Granary Burying Ground in downtown Boston. Only families of the highest social pedigree were entitled to use such symbols on their belongings, architecture, or gravestones. The configuration of the Faneuil family crest is a heart with seven six-pointed stars. (Photograph by Annmarie Rowlands.)

The only extant Faneuil Estate structure is the Gatekeeper's House at the corner of Faneuil and Dunboy Streets. The driveway to the mansion passed in front of this structure, which is believed to be the oldest building in the western part of Allston-Brighton. This photograph dates from about 1925.

The most elaborate Little Cambridge residence was built by wealthy Boston merchant Captain Nathaniel Cunningham about 1730, and stood on the site of Saint Gabriel's Monastery. Destroyed by fire in 1770, it was immediately rebuilt. General Washington dined here in 1775. The Nevins family owned the estate from the 1850s until 1908, when the Passionist Religious Society bought the property. (Courtesy of the Society for the Preservation of New England Antiquities.)

The Bowen-Matchett Mansion stood where Washington and Tip Top Streets presently intersect, west of Oak Square. It was built in the mid-1700s. Daniel Bowen, who acquired the property in 1791, owned Boston's Columbian Museum. The Matchett family bought the house in 1820. Charles H. Matchett, born here, became the 1892 Socialist Labor Party presidential candidate. (Courtesy of the Society for the Preservation of New England Antiquities.)

The Great White Oak, from which Oak Square derives its name, was a remarkable tree. A committee appointed in 1837 to survey the state's botanical and zoological resources found it to be the largest white oak in the commonwealth. An 1845 report noted that "it had probably passed its prime centuries before the first English voice was heard on the shores of Massachusetts." Another description stated: "The cavity of the trunk is capable of sheltering twenty children at one time, as is well known to have been the case." The ancient tree was taken down in the mid-1850s. A measurement just prior to its destruction gave the circumference at the base as nearly 30 feet.

The Colonel Thomas Gardner House, dating from about 1760, stood originally at the corner of Harvard and Brighton Avenues. Colonel Gardner, a leading figure in pre-Revolutionary Massachusetts, was fatally wounded at Bunker Hill. The town of Gardner, Massachusetts, was named in his memory. In the 1850s the house was moved to Higgins Street, near Union Square, where it still stands.

Colonel Thomas Gardner of Little Cambridge was the second highest-ranking American officer killed at the Battle of Bunker Hill. Here we have an engraving of John Trumbull's famous painting, *The Death of General Warren at the Battle of Bunker Hill*. Trumbull, the so-called "painter of the American Revolution," identified each person in the work. The prone figure at the extreme bottom right of the painting represents Colonel Gardner.

Two

Cattle Market

The character of Little Cambridge changed dramatically in 1776, when local entrepreneurs Jonathan Winship I and II, father and son, put out a call to the farmers of the interior towns to send livestock to Little Cambridge to help supply the Continental Army, then headquartered across the Charles River in Cambridge proper. As the livestock arrived, the Winships purchased and slaughtered the animals to feed Washington's hungry troops. With the siege of Boston ended in March 1776, Little Cambridge continued to serve as a collecting point for livestock and as a slaughtering center, with nearby Boston as its principal market.

The town's cattle and slaughtering industries quickly assumed a dominant role in the political life of the community. Feeling that the parent town was doing too little to protect its interests (Cambridge's failure to make critical transportation improvements generated much discontent), the cattle dealers and butchers of Little Cambridge spearheaded a movement for separation from the parent community. In 1807, the Massachusetts legislature authorized the establishment of the independent town of Brighton.

The Brighton Cattle Market was one of the great institutions of nineteenth-century New England. On market day drovers, cattlemen, horse dealers, and peddlers converged on Brighton from every direction. Many hotels were established to accommodate these patrons. The most important of these establishments was the hundred-room Cattle Fair Hotel in Brighton Center, built in 1830, the largest hostelry on the periphery of Boston. The stockyards stood behind the Cattle Fair Hotel for more than a half-century.

The largest fair in Massachusetts, the Brighton Fair and Cattle Show, was held in Brighton every October from 1816 to 1836. The Massachusetts Society for Promoting Agriculture laid out fairgrounds on "Agricultural Hill" (the site of the present Winship School) on the south side of Brighton Center, a stone's throw from the Cattle Fair Hotel.

The building of the Boston & Worcester Railroad through Brighton in 1834 reinforced the town's position as New England's leading cattle and slaughtering center and stimulated its industrial development. By 1860, Brighton contained more than forty small-scale slaughterhouses as well as a score of industrial plants producing tallow, oil, lampblack, varnish, whips, bone fertilizer, and other animal by-products. The small town's yearly manufacturing output stood at an impressive $10 million by 1860, almost one-quarter that of Boston.

While the cattle and slaughtering trades were Brighton's major nineteenth-century industries, horticulture and market gardening were also very important. The leading horticultural establishments included Winship's Gardens in North Brighton; J.L.L.F. Warren's Nonantum Vale Gardens at the corner of Lake and Washington Streets; Breck's Nursery in Oak Square; and Horace Gray's Grapery (later owned by William C. Strong) on Nonantum Hill. Breck and Strong both served as presidents of the Massachusetts Horticultural Society. By the middle of the nineteenth century, Brighton had become one of the two leading horticultural centers near Boston.

The original Little Cambridge Cattle Market was established in 1776 on the grounds of the Bull's Head Tavern, the community's oldest hostelry, which stood on the site of 201 Washington Street about quarter of a mile east of Brighton Center. The tavern, which dated from the mid-1700s, also served as a stop on the Boston to Worcester stagecoach line.

The Winship Mansion, built in 1780, home of the founders of the cattle market, stood on the site of the Brighton Police Station. It was described as being "surrounded by a large tract of highly cultivated land; besides well-stocked pastures, on which grazed many varieties of cattle." In 1820, Samuel Dudley converted the mansion into the Brighton Hotel.

24

One of the first projects undertaken by the newly-created Town of Brighton was the construction of a new and expanded church to replace the cramped 1744 meetinghouse. This building, like its predecessor, stood at the northeast corner of Washington and Market Streets.

Here we have an interior view of the 1808 edifice of the First Church of Brighton.

$30 REWARD.
Stolen from the Sta-

ble in Brighton, on Wednesday, the 15th inst. a light sorrel Horse, saddle, bridle and martingale. The horse was 7 or 8 years old, switch tail and carries it one side, has a little of the spring halt in his off hind leg; a pleasant saddle horse, natural to canter, no particular mark recollected, middling size; an oldish saddle, and the bridle has plated bits and double reins, martingale with plated hooks and tipped with nails. It is supposed that the thief claimed him in the crowd at the stable as his own, and that he went immediately to Boston, as a horse of his description was seen on the Mill Dam, rode by a young man from 16 to 18 years of age. The above reward will be paid for the horse and thief, or $15 for either, and all necessary charges.

Munnis Kenny.
George Cooper.

Brighton, Oct. 18th, 1823.

A $15 reward was offered in 1823 for the capture of a thief and the return of a horse stolen from Brighton. The cattle market attracted large numbers of strangers, and this fostered a rowdy atmosphere in which heavy drinking, carousing, gambling, fighting, reckless driving, and horse thievery were commonplace.

BRIGHTON
CATTLE FAIR HOTEL,

BY ZACHARIAH B. PORTER.

The accommodations of this House are upon the most extensive scale, it has been arranged with particular attention to the *Traveller and Drover*, both as to comfort and convenience.

** *Cotillion Parties, Engine Companies, Clubs, and all Associations*, provided for at instant notice. The Larder will always be provided with the best the seasons afford, and the Bar, as well as every part of the House, will be attended to with strict reference to the comfort, convenience, and satisfaction of the patrons of this Establishment.**

Brighton's largest hotel, the Cattle Fair, opened in 1830. It was situated on the north side of Washington Street, between Market and Parsons Streets. Containing some one hundred rooms, a dining room that could accommodate as many as four to five hundred guests at a sitting, and a grand ballroom, it was the largest hotel outside of Boston and attracted much upper-class patronage. The hotel's first manager, Zachariah B. Porter, later founded the Porter House Hotel in Cambridge, from which Porter Square and the porterhouse steak derived their names. The porticoed building to the left was the original headquarters of the Bank of Brighton, which was founded in 1832 chiefly to handle the business of the burgeoning Brighton Cattle Market.

In the nineteenth century, banks printed their own paper currency. A bank existed in Brighton as early as 1828 for the convenience of the patrons of the cattle market. This $20 bank note was issued by the Bank of Brighton in 1850. Its motifs include the cattle trade, the railroad, and a female figure symbolizing farming.

New stockyards were laid out to the rear of the Cattle Fair Hotel in 1830, replacing the original yards at the Bull's Head Tavern. The raised structure at the center of the grounds was an auctioneer's platform. The stockyards extended back to the vicinity of present-day Bennett Street.

This engraving depicts Brighton Center as it looked in 1832. By the 1830s, as many as six thousand head of cattle were being driven into the market town each week from points as far away as Maine, New Hampshire, and Vermont.

The Baldwin & Murdock grocery, Brighton's oldest store, was established in 1811 on the site of the present Warren Building (329-343 Washington Street) in Brighton Center. In 1830 the store was acquired by William Warren, who converted it into a combination drug store, grocery, and depot for the sale of school supplies.

In 1852 the Cattle Fair Hotel was extensively remodeled by noted architect William Washburn in the popular Italianate style. A fourth story, a portico of rusticated stone, and verandas were

added. This illustration, which appeared in *Ballou's Pictorial* in June 1856, depicts the grounds of the Cattle Fair Hotel as they appeared on Market Day.

These engravings, *Going to Market* and *Road Scene in Brighton*, were published in 1852. An accompanying article noted, "Thursday is market-day [in Brighton], and for several days previous, the roads are thronged with droves of cattle and sheep. . . . The sales for several years have amounted to between two and three million dollars per annum, and the number of cattle to two to three hundred thousand annually."

This bill of fare was presented at the Cattle Fair Hotel Dining Room on January 4, 1860.

By the 1860s there were over forty slaughterhouses in Brighton. One of the local butchers, Gustavus Franklin Swift, later founded the Swift Meatpacking Company in Chicago. Swift lived on Brighton's Oakland Street in 1870. The location of his local slaughterhouse is uncertain. This illustration was furnished by the Swift Meatpacking Company.

Captain Jonathan Winship III and his brother, Captain Nathan, played a key role in the development of the American Pacific trade. In 1818, Captain Jonathan returned to Brighton and founded Winship's Gardens, the community's first horticultural business, thus inaugurating Brighton's second great nineteenth-century industry.

Breck's Nursery, another leading Brighton horticultural business, was established in 1854 at the northwest corner of Tremont and Nonantum Streets in Oak Square. It stood behind the residence of its owner Joseph Breck, on the land now occupied by the Oak Square School.

This Joseph Breck & Sons seed catalog dates from the mid-nineteenth century. Breck was perhaps the foremost Massachusetts horticulturist of his day. The author of an outstanding treatise, *The Young Florist, or Conversations on the Culture of Flowers and on Natural History*, he arrived in Brighton in 1836 from Lancaster, Massachusetts, having served as superintendent of the horticultural gardens there. He was also editor of the *New England Farmer*, the state's leading agricultural journal. Breck's first Brighton nursery was located at the corner of Washington and Allston Streets, near the Brookline boundary. Breck also operated a large agricultural supply business in Boston, near Faneuil Hall, and served as president of the Massachusetts Horticultural Society from 1859 to 1862.

William C. Strong's glass-enclosed grapery on Nonantum Hill was an important local landmark. At the height of its operation, it was one of the largest vineyards in the country. Strong also cultivated fruit trees and flowers. In 1855 he excavated Chandler's Pond for ice-cutting. He served as president of the Massachusetts Horticultural Society from 1871 to 1874.

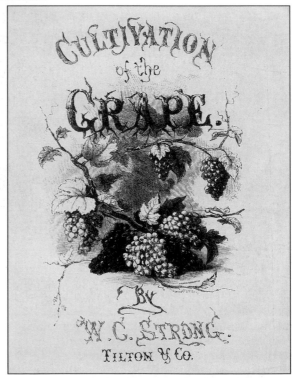

Here we have the title page of Strong's principal work, *Cultivation of the Grape*.

Novelist Sarah Willis Eldredge, whose pen name was "Fanny Fern," resided in Brighton with her banker husband, Charles Eldredge, from 1837 to 1846. When his death left her almost penniless with three children to support, she began writing and soon gained great popularity. Her most important novel, *Ruth Hall*, was based on her Brighton experiences.

Ice-cutting was an important industry in nineteenth-century Brighton. This wintertime photograph shows an ice house on Brooks Pond, viewed from Brooks Street. Located in the vicinity of present-day Hobart Street, Brooks Pond was filled in the 1890s for the residential development of present-day Bothwell, Newcastle, and Donnybrook Roads.

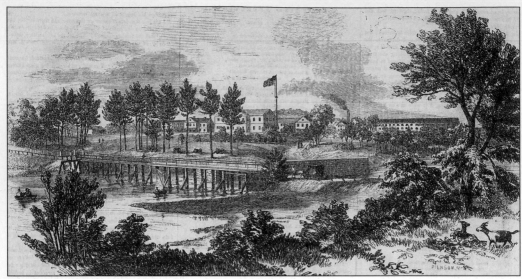

Many Brighton residents worked at the nearby Watertown Arsenal. This 1854 engraving from *Gleason's Pictorial* shows the North Beacon Street Bridge connecting Brighton and Watertown. The arsenal complex lies in the background.

In April 1865, the people of Brighton celebrated the end of the Civil War in a ceremony held outside of the Cattle Fair Hotel in Brighton Center.

Brighton's many hotels, but especially the Brighton Hotel and the Cattle Fair, were popular destinations for Bostonians who owned private sleighs and carriages. Here we have summer and winter views of visitors leaving the Brighton Hotel (which stood on the site of the present District 14 Police Station) to return home via the Mill Dam.

This engraving of sleighing outside of the Cattle Fair Hotel in the 1850s was the work of the great illustrator and painter Winslow Homer.

The Cattle Fair Hotel is shown as it appeared about 1895, just before its demolition.

Three

Civic Center

Brighton was a pioneer in many areas of government service. Its dominant cattle dealers, slaughterhouse proprietors, market gardeners, and horticulturists sought to offset their community's rough-and-tumble image by providing a broad range of high quality public facilities and services.

An elaborate Greek Revival-style town hall was erected in 1841, symbolic of the town's flourishing commercial economy. Well-built schoolhouses were constructed; by 1873 the school system included a high school on Academy Hill, north and south grammar schools, and six primary schools. Brighton High School, which opened in 1841, was among the first high schools in the Boston area. From 1841 to 1843, the market town ranked ahead of all other cities and towns in Massachusetts in per capita spending on public education.

In 1864 Brighton founded one of the area's earliest public libraries. Private subscription libraries had existed in town since 1828. James Holton's 1863 bequest of $5,000 for the purchase of books prompted the town fathers to establish a public library. By 1873, Brighton's ten-thousand-volume collection was housed in the Holton Library, an elaborate Victorian-Gothic-style edifice on Academy Hill Road. Designed by Brighton-born architect George Fuller, and named in honor of the aforementioned benefactor, the Holton Library was perhaps the finest public building Brighton constructed in its sixty-seven-year history as an independent town.

The town invested heavily in fire protection, constructing substantial buildings for its volunteer fire companies, and providing them with the most up-to-date equipment. Fires were, of course, a major hazard in this commercial and industrial center.

In addition, Brighton was one of only a handful of Massachusetts communities to establish an elaborate "rural-style" public cemetery, Evergreen, patterned after the Mount Auburn Cemetery in Cambridge. The town's horticulturists were particularly active in promoting this ambitious project.

Brighton's town government fell short, however, in the protection of the public health, the maintenance of roadways and drainage, and the establishment of an adequate police force, all public services that the cattle and slaughtering interests regarded as potentially damaging to their trade. Any proposal that threatened the profitability of these key lines of trade—the great engine of the local economy—was given short shrift by the town fathers. As Brighton's population mounted in the mid-1800s, the problems associated with waste disposal became particularly severe. By the late 1860s, it had the highest mortality rate of any town near Boston. Not until 1870–73 did the community begin to confront these problems head on.

The tradition of heavy investment in public facilities survived Brighton's annexation to Boston in 1874. The city continued to construct handsome public edifices—schools, fire stations, a police station, and a courthouse—adding appreciably to Allston-Brighton's rich architectural legacy.

The Brighton town seal was adopted in the mid-1860s, in Brighton's last decade as an independent town. Designed by Reverend Frederic A. Whitney of Brighton's First Church, it featured a greenhouse motif, symbolic of the town's second most important industry, horticulture and market gardening.

The Brighton Town Hall stood at the northeast corner of Washington Street and Waldo Terrace in Brighton Center. Built in 1841 by local master-carpenter Granville Fuller, and designed by architect Richard Bond, this elaborate Greek Revival-style edifice reflected the town's prosperity in the pre-Civil War era. After Brighton's annexation to Boston, the building served as a local courthouse and jail. It later housed various veterans' organizations, including a local GAR post. Acquired by the Knights of Columbus in the 1960s, the structure was extensively damaged by fire in 1977 and demolished. The granite basement of the old town hall was incorporated into the building that replaced it, the Brighton Knights of Columbus Hall.

The original Oak Square School, built in 1832, stood in the shadow of the Great White Oak at the center of Oak Square, on the site of the present Oak Square Common.

In 1855, following the removal of the Great White Oak, a larger Oak Square School was built at the same location. This photograph was taken about 1880, looking northeast toward Faneuil Street from Tremont Street. When the present Oak Square School was built, the 1855 structure was moved, enlarged, and converted into a residence. The building still stands at 16 Bigelow Street.

In 1894, the present Oak Square School was built at 35 Nonantum Street, designed by City Architect Edmund March Wheelwright. The Boston Landmarks Commission designated this handsome Neoclassical building (Boston's last wooden schoolhouse) as a City of Boston Architectural and Historical Landmark in 1979. In 1981, it was converted into condominiums by the Allston-Brighton Community Development Corporation.

Here we have an 1899 class photograph from the Oak Square School.

Brighton was among the first area towns to establish a public high school. The original Brighton High School stood at the upper end of Academy Hill Road, opposite the Rushmore Road intersection. The building pictured here was the third to occupy the site, dating from 1868.

The old Brighton High School is visible at the upper end of Academy Hill Road in this 1890 panoramic view.

In 1889, Brighton High School's graduating class contained a total of just fifteen students, five males and ten females. Longtime headmaster Benjamin Wormelle and three female faculty members (all seated) appear in the photograph, which was taken outside the high school building.

By 1894 Allston-Brighton's fast-growing population prompted the city to construct a new Brighton High School at the corner of Warren and Cambridge Streets (the present Taft Middle School). Designed by Edmund March Wheelwright, this edifice has been described as "nationally influential."

The Bennett Grammar School, named for prominent cattle dealer Stephen Hastings Bennett and designed by J. Foster Ober, was built in 1873 on Chestnut Hill Avenue facing Wilson Park. It was one of three neighboring elaborate Victorian Gothic structures that the town built in its last year of independence. The building, which still stands (minus its distinctive mansard roof), now serves as a center for Russian Jewish immigrants. The photograph, which dates from 1900, shows a house (on the far left) that was removed in 1910 to connect Dighton Street with Chestnut Hill Avenue. Also visible to the right of that house is the cupola of the old Bennett Grammar School, which stood on the site of the present Winship Elementary School.

The Washington Allston School, dating from 1878, stood on the south side of Cambridge Street just west of the Harvard Avenue intersection. It was the first major public facility built in Allston-Brighton after its annexation by the City of Boston in 1874. Damaged by fire, it was demolished in 1977.

The Gardner Elementary School, at 30 Athol Street in North Allston, was built in 1905 to replace the wooden Everett Elementary School. The older building, dating from 1872, is visible to the rear of the new edifice. It was designed by noted Brighton architect George Fuller. The first public kindergarten in Boston was established in the Everett Elementary School in 1873, but was discontinued shortly after Brighton's annexation to Boston. (Courtesy of the Society for the Preservation of New England Antiquities.)

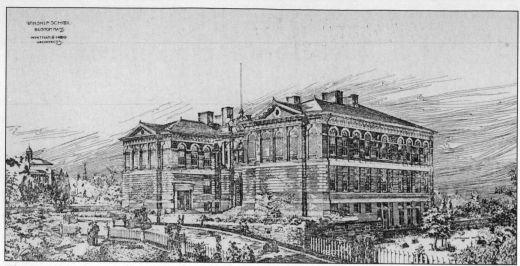

The Winship Elementary School at 54 Dighton Street near Brighton Center was built in 1899 on a design of architects Whitman & Hodd. In the 1920s, a fourth story was added. The school was named for J.P.C. Winship, local historian and long-time member of the Boston School Committee.

The Shingle-style Aberdeen Elementary School was built in the late 1890s at 186 Chestnut Hill Avenue. In the mid-1920s, the city sold the property to American Legion Post 17. This photograph dates from the 1930s.

Allston-Brighton also contains many Catholic schools. Saint Columbkille's Parochial School, situated behind Saint Columbkille's Church on Arlington Street, opened in 1901. It was designed by noted ecclesiastical architect F. Joseph Untersee. (Courtesy of the Society for the Preservation of New England Antiquities.)

The Brighton High School Cadet Corps is shown outside the 1894 school building (now Taft Middle School) about 1900.

The Holton Library, built in 1873, stood at 40 Academy Hill Road, the site of the present Brighton Library. Designed by George Fuller, the library was named for its benefactor, James Holton. It was demolished by the City of Boston in 1969. The house to the right belonged to prominent slaughterhouse proprietor Nathaniel Jackson. (Courtesy of the Society for the Preservation of New England Antiquities.)

This image shows the Holton Library foyer with a view of the main reading room in 1968.

Here we see the main reading room of the Holton Library in 1968.

The children's room of the Holton Library was also photographed in 1968.

This fire station, built in 1873 and designed by Abel C. Martin, stood on Chestnut Hill Avenue just outside of Brighton Center on the site of the Veronica Smith Senior Center. Here were housed Engine Company No. 29 and Ladder Company No. 11 of the Boston Fire Department. The photograph dates from the late 1870s. It is one of a large collection of photographs of fire stations and fire apparatus kindly donated to the Brighton-Allston Historical Society by John McLane of Allston.

This view of the Chestnut Hill Avenue Fire Station shows firefighters and horse-drawn apparatus in 1902. The building was destroyed by fire in the late 1930s. In the early 1940s, its shell was incorporated into the Brighton Municipal Building, which was later converted into the Veronica Smith Senior Center.

Ladder Company 11 is shown here about 1900 outside the Bennett Grammar School. (McLane Collection.)

The old wooden Harvard Avenue Fire Station, at 16 Harvard Avenue, Allston, is shown here about 1880. It was housed Chemical Engine No. 6 of the Boston Fire Department. (McLane Collection.)

This photograph shows Engine Company No. 41 outside the Harvard Avenue Fire Station in 1915. In 1891 this new brick structure replaced the older wooden fire station. (McLane Collection.)

In 1888 this Richardsonian Romanesque-style fire station was built at 444 Western Avenue in North Brighton. Engine Company No. 34 has assembled outside of the building in this 1913 photograph. (McLane Collection.)

Four
Streetcar Suburb

Though linked to the metropolis by rail from an early date, Allston-Brighton attracted few commuters before the 1870s. Its industries were so noxious and its local government so wedded to the interests of the livestock trade, that Bostonians looking for pleasant suburban settings naturally chose other locales.

Only in the 1870 to 1874 period did Allston-Brighton begin its transformation from a market town to a commuter suburb. This occurred when a group of local businessmen led by State Senator William Wirt Warren, having concluded that residential development offered much greater profit potential than the livestock trade, took over the town government and pushed through a series of reforms that fundamentally reshaped the character of the community.

These reforms included the consolidation of Allston-Brighton's forty-plus slaughterhouses into a single, modern facility, or abattoir, and the relocation of Brighton Center's sprawling cattle yards. Both enterprises were placed in already-industrialized North Brighton, close to the railroad and the tidal Charles River. By virtue of these measures, hundreds of acres of previously fouled land were opened to high-quality residential development.

In addition, the Warren faction pushed through a major and costly public works program that improved roads, sewerage, buildings, parks, and street lighting. The city planners even suggested that a second railroad be built through the central part of Brighton, but this project never materialized.

Calculating that higher property taxes would only serve to discourage commuters, Brighton actually lowered its real property tax in the early 1870s. While generating only $500,000 of income in the 1870 to 1873 period, the town spent $1.5 million on its public improvements program, borrowing the rest at high rates of interest. Members of the Warren faction took advantage of this spending frenzy and sold property to the town at inflated prices. Thus the town's debt increased eightfold in just four years.

When the City of Boston sought to annex Brighton in October 1873, the annexationists (once again Senator Warren and his faction) were able to argue that absorption by Boston would mean relatively low taxes (since the wealthy metropolis would absorb Brighton's heavy debt), while continued independence would mean significantly higher taxes, slowed development, and depressed property values. The town's electorate found this line of reasoning highly compelling, and on October 7, 1873, sanctioned annexation to the City of Boston by a four-to-one margin, the highest rate of approval annexation received in any Boston suburb. Thus, on the first Monday of January 1874, Brighton became a part of the City of Boston.

The parts of Brighton that experienced the earliest suburban development were those that enjoyed the readiest access to public transportation. The eastern section underwent especially rapid growth. This area had been given the name Allston in 1867, after the great painter Washington Allston (1779-1843), who had once lived in nearby Cambridgeport. Allston is the only community in the United States named for a painter.

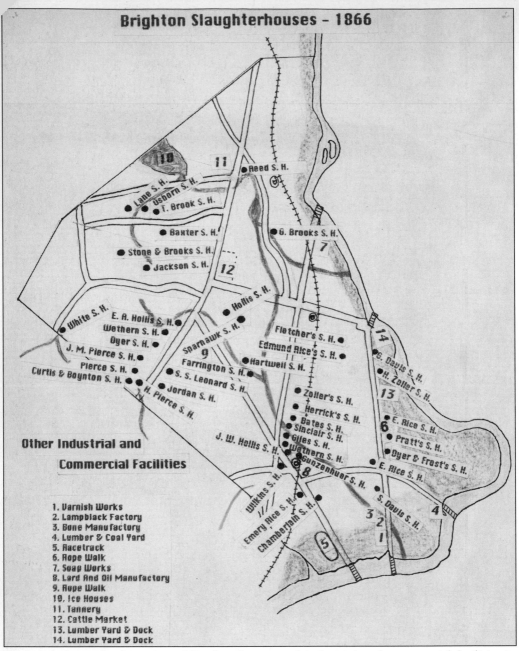

Brighton Slaughterhouses – 1866

Reed S. H.

Lane S. H.
Usborn S. H.
T. Brook S. H.

Baxter S. H.
G. Brooks S. H.

Stone & Brooks S. H.

Jackson S. H.

White S. H.
E. A. Hollis S. H.
Wethern S. H.
Dyer S. H.
J. M. Pierce S. H.
Pierce S. H.
Curtis & Boynton S. H.
H. Pierce S. H.
Sparhawk S. H.
Farrington S. H.
S. S. Leonard S. H.
Jordan S. H.
Hollis S. H.

Fletcher's S. H.
Edmund Rice's S. H.
Hartwell S. H.

Zoller's S. H.
Herrick's S. H.
Bates S. H.
Sinclair S. H.
Giles S. H.
Wethern S. H.
Gunzenhuer S. H.

J. W. Hollis S. H.

Wilkins S. H.
Emery Rice S. H.
Chamberlain S. H.

G. Davis S. H.
H. Zoller S. H.

E. Rice S. H.
Pratt's S. H.
Dyer & Frost's S. H.
E. Rice S. H.

S. Davis S. H.

Other Industrial and Commercial Facilities

1. Varnish Works
2. Lampblack Factory
3. Bone Manufactory
4. Lumber & Coal Yard
5. Racetrack
6. Rope Walk
7. Soap Works
8. Lard And Oil Manufactory
9. Rope Walk
10. Ice Houses
11. Tannery
12. Cattle Market
13. Lumber Yard & Dock
14. Lumber Yard & Dock

This map shows the locations of Brighton's principal industrial and commercial facilities in 1866. The cattle market (no. 12) was the central element, but forty-one slaughterhouses, mostly small-scale (none capitalized at more than $50,000), also dotted the landscape. In addition, Brighton contained a varnish works, lampblack factory, bone fertilizer plant, soap works, lard and tallow manufactory, tannery, ice houses, ropewalks, lumber and coal yards, and a race track—Beacon Park—on the site of the present Massachusetts Turnpike entrance in Allston. The slaughterhouses, though scattered, required natural drainage. Most were therefore located near the tidal Charles River or near a brook or stream that flowed into the river.

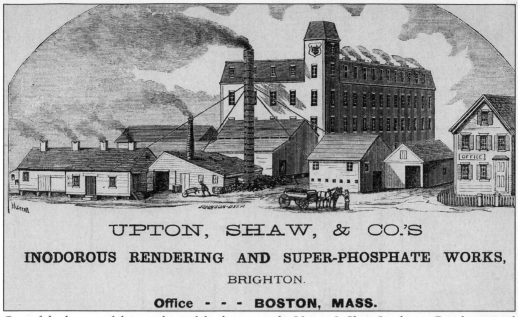

UPTON, SHAW, & CO.'S

INODOROUS RENDERING AND SUPER-PHOSPHATE WORKS,

BRIGHTON.

Office - - - BOSTON, MASS.

One of the largest of these industrial facilities was the Upton & Shaw Inodorous Rendering and Super Phosphate Works, which manufactured bone fertilizer. It was located on the south side of Western Avenue, some 500 feet east of the North Harvard Street intersection.

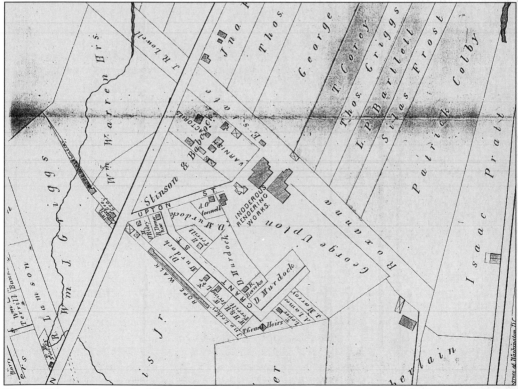

This 1875 map shows the Upton & Shaw bone fertilizer works and several other neighboring industrial facilities, including the Stimson & Babcock varnish factory and two ropewalks.

Brighton gained a magnificent visual and recreational amenity in 1870 with the construction of the Chestnut Hill Reservoir in the southeastern corner of the town. The gate was located at the Chestnut Hill Avenue entrance to the Reservoir. A magnificent driveway, varying in width from 60 to 80 feet, surrounded the entire facility.

The reservoir served as a storage facility for the Cochituate Water Works, Boston's water supply system. Its two basins had a capacity of 800 million gallons. The reservoir gate is visible just right of center. While the reservoir was a popular location for pleasure driving, the surrounding area failed to experience much residential development due to the odors emanating from two nearby slaughterhouses.

This engraving shows the driveway that surrounded the smaller of the Chestnut Hill Reservoir's two basins, the Lawrence Basin, named for the great industrialist Amos A. Lawrence, whose residence sat on the heights now occupied by Boston College. The Lawrence Basin was deeded to the college and filled in 1950, and is now the site of the university's lower campus.

This gatehouse, situated on Beacon Street just south of the Chestnut Hill Avenue intersection, was one of three such structures on the margin of the reservoir.

State Senator William Wirt Warren spearheaded the drive to transform Brighton from a market town to a streetcar suburb by shepherding the abattoir bill through the legislature and by convincing the town to borrow heavily to improve its infrastructure. A promising political career was cut short by Warren's early death in 1880 at age forty-six. (Courtesy of Dr. Lyman O. Warren.)

Hotelkeeper George Wilson was a member of the Warren faction. When the town purchased his Brighton Hotel for an enormous $70,000 in 1873, the *Boston Daily Advertiser* charged that a corrupt "ring," worse than New York City's Tammany Hall, had systematically defrauded the little town of Brighton in the 1870 to 1873 period.

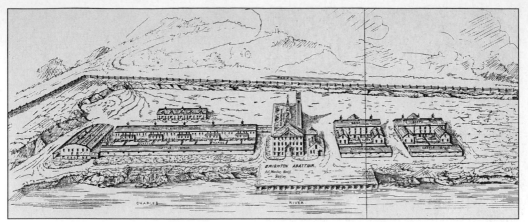

The consolidation of all of Brighton's slaughterhouses into a single, modern facility by the Butcher's Slaughtering and Melting Association, or Brighton Abattoir, removed a major obstacle to Brighton's rise as a streetcar suburb. The abattoir was situated on the Charles River, between the North Beacon Street and Arsenal Street Bridges. It was constructed in 1872.

This panoramic photograph of the abattoir complex, taken from the Watertown side of the Charles River, dates from 1912. The houses on the hill in the background stood on Wexford Street, a discontinued roadway that ran parallel to the present Leo Birmingham Parkway.

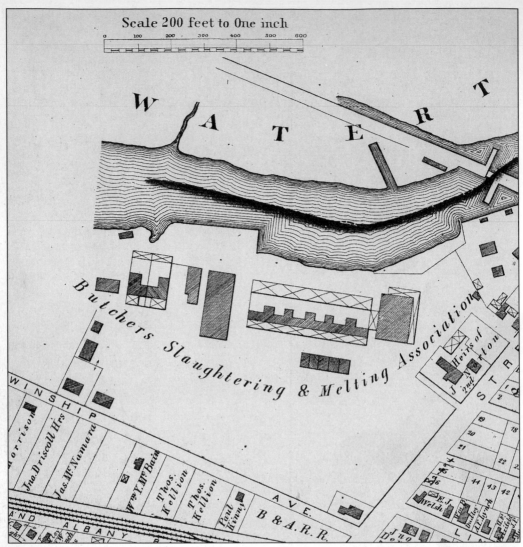

WATER

Butchers Slaughtering & Melting Association

WINSHIP

Morrison

Jno. Driscoll Hrs

Jas. McNamara

Wm. T. McBain

Thos. Kellion

Thos. Kellion

Paul Kinny

AVE.

B & A. R. R.

ALBAND

STR

Heirs of J. Newton

E. J. Welsh

This 1875 map of the abattoir complex shows the facility as it first appeared. By 1890 it resembled an industrial village. The 60-acre complex had 1,000 feet of frontage on the Charles River, allowing schooners and sloops to tie up at its wharves. Its buildings included a large rendering house and fourteen slaughterhouses, ten of which were arranged under one continuous roof. Under the building ran a cement cellar in which the blood, tallow, feet, offal, and other portions of the slaughtered animals were allowed to accumulate in iron wheelbarrows, which were taken to the rendering houses to be transformed into oil, tallow, and fertilizer.

The Brighton Stockyards, which were originally located behind the Cattle Fair Hotel in Brighton Center, moved to North Brighton in 1881. They stood on the site of the present Honeywell Bull plant. The long brick building to the rear in this 1950s photograph was the Boston & Albany Railroad's paint shop.

So important was the livestock trade to the Boston & Albany Railroad that a special station and loading platform were established for the Brighton Stockyards (left center). The Market Street Bridge and the Brighton Depot are visible further down the tracks. (Courtesy of the Society for the Preservation of New England Antiquities.)

Despite the shift towards residential development, much of Allston-Brighton remained essentially industrial. This 1912 view of lower Cambridge Street from Magazine Beach, Cambridge, shows the Boston Consolidated Gas Company plant on the site now occupied by the Doubletree Quarters Suites Hotel.

Major changes were made along the Charles River shore between Market Street and Cambridge Street at the turn of the century. A mile long raceway, the Charles River Speedway, opened here in 1899. This 1902 photograph shows hundreds of sulkies gathered on the riverside course for the third annual "Speedway Parade."

Horticulture continued to be a major business in late-nineteenth-century Brighton. In 1884 William C. Strong sold his Brighton greenhouses, situated on the southern slope of Nonantum Hill facing Kenrick Street, to William Elliott. Elliott improved and reconditioned the greenhouses. Here he grew a wide variety of flowers and vegetables.

The Brighton Five Cents Savings Bank and the Brighton Bakery were located at 326-328 Washington Street, on the site of the present Brighton Elks Hall. This photograph dates from about 1885.

The Benjamin F. Pierce House at the corner of Washington Street and Nantasket Avenue typifies the residences built by Brighton's cattle dealers and slaughterhouse proprietors when cattle was king in Brighton. It was constructed in 1834 by cattle dealer and long-time selectman Benjamin F. Pierce. Later it was owned by A.J. Furbush, who operated a hack and livery stable. (Courtesy of the Society for the Preservation of New England Antiquities.)

This 1905 view of Washington Street in Brighton Center looking west from the vicinity of Waldo Terrace contains two landmarks that have disappeared. The building behind the lamppost to the left was Brighton's general store. The mansard-roofed Victorian Gothic building behind it, at the Chestnut Hill Avenue intersection, was the headquarters of the National Bank of Brighton.

This later photograph of Brighton Center, dating from 1915, shows the newly built commercial block (on the right) at the intersection of Washington and Market Streets.

This photograph of Brighton Center dates from 1910. The wooden building (right center) is Agricultural Hall (1819), formerly the headquarters of the Massachusetts Society for Promoting Agriculture. The structure (now Brighton Travel) was removed from Agricultural Hill (site of the Winship School) about 1840. Notice also the distinctive balustrade atop the Washington or Rourke Building, which is now missing. (Courtesy of the Society for the Preservation of New England Antiquities.)

The residence of Life Baldwin (president of the National Market Bank) at 11 Sparhawk Street epitomizes the high-quality suburban architecture that dominated many areas of Allston-Brighton at the turn of the century. This photograph was taken around 1890.

The Brighton Avenue Baptist Church stood at the intersection of Brighton Avenue and Cambridge Street in Union Square, Allston, on the site now occupied by the Union Square Fire Station. Built in the mid-1850s, it was destroyed by fire in 1929. This 1915 view shows streetcars on lower Cambridge Street, which were part of a line that ran to Central Square, Cambridge. (Courtesy of the Society for the Preservation of New England Antiquities.)

This western view of Union Square shows Union Hall, an elaborate wooden Italianate structure that once stood at the intersection of Cambridge and North Beacon Streets. Union Hall was built in the 1860s and stood until the late 1960s. The commercial block fronting the hall was constructed just after the turn of the century.

Streetcars ran along Harvard Avenue to a depot on Braintree Street, as shown in this 1910 photograph of Allston Square. The Chester Block (left center), built in 1892, and the adjacent Allston Hall Block, dating from 1890, helped give the square a prosperous appearance. (Courtesy of the Society for the Preservation of New England Antiquities.)

Harvard University helped transform Allston's Charles River shoreline by moving its athletic facilities to Soldier's Field in the 1890s. The removal of the Heaton Coal Company and wharf also encouraged residential development along lower North Harvard Street. By 1916, twelve houses were clustered here (left center), but were demolished in 1925 for the Harvard Business School complex.

With the removal of cattle yards to North Brighton in 1881, the former 6-acre Brighton Center stockyard site experienced rapid residential development. This 1910 photograph of Parsons Street, near Brighton Center, also shows the impact the installation of utility poles had upon the landscape. Notice the relative absence of trees on the right-hand side where poles have been erected. (Courtesy of the Society for the Preservation of New England Antiquities.)

Residential development in Allston was very rapid. This duplex at 35 Linden Street, at the corner of Farrington Street in Allston, was built by local landowner and developer Jesse Tirrell in the 1880s.

The most fashionable street in Allston at the turn of the century was Gardner Street. Originally part of the estate of Revolutionary War hero Colonel Thomas Gardner and named in his memory, the street's residents included Homer Rogers (chairman of the Boston Board of Aldermen and namesake of Brighton's Rogers Park) and Reverend Frederic Augustus Whitney (minister of the First Church of Brighton).

The Oak Square Common is shown here as it appeared about 1900, looking west up Washington Street towards Newton. (Courtesy of the Society for the Preservation of New England Antiquities.)

A commercial block had just been built between Breck Avenue and Nonantum Streets in Oak Square when this photograph was taken in 1910. In addition, the old Breck Mansion at the corner of Nonantum and Tremont Streets has been cleared away to allow for additional commercial development. Rapid residential development of Nonantum (or Breck) Hill occurred between 1910 and 1930. (Courtesy of the Society for the Preservation of New England Antiquities.)

This southwesterly view of Washington Street just above Oak Square was taken from Bigelow Street about 1910. At the center of the photograph are two historical landmarks that were shortly to disappear: the old Champney House (rear view) and the Matchett Mansion.

By 1920 the entire southern end of Bigelow Street had been developed. While the right side of the street experienced development at a very early date (before 1875), as its mansarded roofs suggest, the left side remained entirely undeveloped until the early 1900s.

Oak Square experienced its fastest residential development in the flat area enclosed by Washington and Faneuil Streets. As a result, the north side of Washington Street east of Oak Square became a commercial district. The store on the left, Byrne's Oak Square Market, stood at the corner of Washington and Brackett Streets. (Courtesy of the Society for the Preservation of New England Antiquities.)

Many three-deckers were being built in the Oak Square neighborhood in the 1910 to 1930 period, as exemplified by this photograph of Montfern Avenue taken about 1915 looking north towards Bigelow Hill. (Courtesy of the Society for the Preservation of New England Antiquities.)

Constructed in the 1890s, Commonwealth Avenue did not experience immediate development. This fact is probably a result of the roadway's competition with Beacon Street in Brookline. When large-scale development finally came, however, in the World War I era, it was of a uniformly high order. An excellent example is the Princeton Hotel at 1277 Commonwealth Avenue (a luxury apartment building), designed by the distinguished architect John C. Spofford. (Courtesy of the Society for the Preservation of New England Antiquities.)

The Sutherland Apartments at 1714-1742 Commonwealth Avenue, near the Sutherland Road intersection, are shown here under construction in 1914. This 600-foot long apartment complex is the best example of Jacobethan-style architecture in Allston-Brighton. (Courtesy of the Society for the Preservation of New England Antiquities.)

No single building in Allston-Brighton reflected the community's new suburban character more powerfully than the handsome District 14 Police Station, designed by Edmund March Wheelwight. The station opened in 1894 at the eastern end of Brighton Center on the site of the old Winship Mansion.

This 1938 photograph shows a trolley on Harvard Avenue crossing Commonwealth Avenue on its way to Dudley Station in Roxbury. (Collection of Mel Beaton.)

Five

Transportation Center

Allston-Brighton's location at the western edge of Boston gave it particular importance as a transportation center—a gateway to the metropolis. In the colonial era, two of the main roads connecting Boston to its hinterland (the Roxbury and Watertown Highways) passed through Little Cambridge. The community's location on the Charles River, then a major commercial artery, also gave it distinct transportation advantages. The cattle and slaughtering industries arose in Brighton as a direct product of this gateway location.

Road building and bridge construction projects were matters of deep concern to the market town. Such concerns prompted Little Cambridge to seek political independence in 1807. With the building of the Roxbury Mill Dam across the Back Bay in 1821 and the Mill Dam Extension into Brighton in 1822, the town was provided with an even more direct link to the city.

A major transportation development came in 1834 with the construction of the Boston & Worcester Railroad through the northern section of the community. The B&W reinforced Brighton's position as the great regional cattle and slaughtering center. It also greatly stimulated industrial and commercial development. The railroad, in turn, profited handsomely from the cattle trade. At mid-century its Brighton Depot was generating more income than its much larger Boston Depot, most of it deriving, of course, from livestock shipments. In the 1865 to 1900 period, the line (renamed the Boston & Albany) expanded its local facilities by adding extensive car repair and paint shops, a freight yard, two round houses, and loading facilities, all located in Allston. By the 1860s the railroad was the single largest taxpayer and employer in Allston-Brighton.

The railway system became as important to individual residents as it was to industry, especially after 1874. As early as 1858, the community was served by a horse railway line that ran from Newton to Boston via Oak Square, Brighton Center, Cambridge Street, Central Square, and the West Boston (now Longfellow) Bridge. By the late nineteenth century, many Allston-Brighton residents were commuting to work in Boston by train. In the 1880s, the Boston & Albany replaced the wooden Allston, Brighton, and Faneuil Depots with handsome stone edifices designed by the renowned architect Henry Hobson Richardson. Sadly, only one of these structures, the Allston Depot, still survives.

It was the more efficient electric streetcar, however, that had the greatest developmental impact on Allston-Brighton. The first electric streetcar ride in Boston originated from a station on Braintree Street in Allston on December 31, 1888. The electric streetcar unleashed a second and far more intensive tide of residential development.

Another transportation-related development, which occurred in the 1908 to 1912 period, was the transformation of the tidal Charles, once lined with wharves and industrial facilities, into the great recreational resource it has become in our time. This was accomplished by the construction of a dam at the mouth of the Charles River, and the systematic improvement of the Allston-Brighton shoreline in the years that followed.

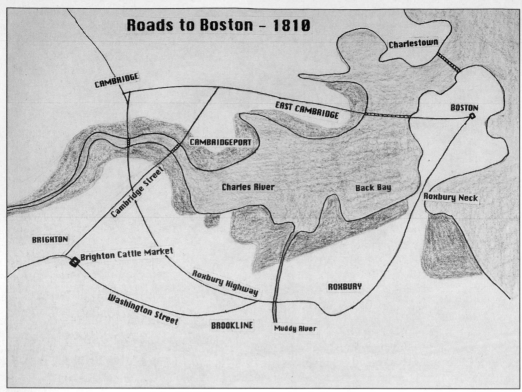

Roads to Boston – 1810

Charlestown

CAMBRIDGE

EAST CAMBRIDGE

BOSTON

CAMBRIDGEPORT

Cambridge Street

Charles River

Back Bay

Roxbury Neck

BRIGHTON

Brighton Cattle Market

Roxbury Highway

ROXBURY

Washington Street

BROOKLINE   Muddy River

Prior to the construction of the Mill Dam across the Back Bay, the shortest route from Brighton to Boston, some 4 miles long, was a northern approach by way of Cambridge Street, Cambridgeport, and the West Boston (or Longfellow) Bridge. The southern, or overland route, by way of Brookline, Roxbury, and the Roxbury Neck, was twice as long.

The Mill Dam Road (1821), present Beacon Street, provided a shorter route to the city. This photograph was taken from the roof of the Massachusetts State House in 1858. The Mill Dam is at the extreme right, with the hills of Brighton visible in the upper right-hand corner.

The 1824 Mill Dam Road Extension through Brookline and Brighton, known as the Brighton Road, was a fashionable gathering-place for the owners of fast horses. In these quaint old prints, dating from 1872, we see the youngbloods of Boston on their way to and from the so-called "Trot."

Brighton Station.

Rail transportation between Brighton and Boston was established in 1834. Here we have an engraving of the original Brighton Depot of the Boston & Worcester Railroad, situated in Winship's Garden in North Brighton. An elaborate, 37-acre formal terraced garden adorned with flowers and shrubs, it contained a 100-foot long conservatory and arbors where weary railroad passengers could rest.

Later in the century, the Brighton Depot was moved to a point just east of the Market Street Bridge. In the mid-1880s, the Boston & Albany Railroad built an elaborate stone edifice designed by H.H. Richardson to replace the original wooden depot. This building was demolished in the 1950s.

The Allston Depot, built in 1886 and designed by H.H. Richardson, is the only surviving Allston-Brighton railroad depot.

The Boston & Albany Railroad owned extensive facilities in Allston-Brighton, as shown in this 1915 photograph looking west from the Cambridge Street Bridge. Diagonally across the tracks from the Allston Depot stood the B&A Car Repair Shops, occupying six buildings.

This 1905 photograph, looking north from Bigelow Hill, shows the Faneuil Depot (center), the North Beacon Street Bridge, and various buildings of the Watertown Arsenal. The large building to the right is the Rivett Lathe & Grinder Manufacturing Company on Riverview Road. The mansarded double houses in the foreground, dating from the early 1870s, still stand on Newton Street.

The original Faneuil Depot, a wooden structure, was built in the early 1870s on Brooks Street. In the late 1880s it was replaced by this handsome Richardsonian Romanesque edifice, which was demolished in 1962 for the Massachusetts Turnpike Extension. (Courtesy of the Society for the Preservation of New England Antiquities.)

This 1892 photograph of the Cambridge Street Bridge under construction shows the Dupee Estate, which the B&A Railroad later incorporated into its massive Allston freight yard. The houses to the right line the northern side of Pratt Street. (Courtesy of the Society for the Preservation of New England Antiquities.)

This view taken from the same vantage point as the previous photograph shows how extensive the Allston freight yard had become by 1900. The freight yard reached its maximum growth in the late 1920s when it contained nearly a hundred parallel tracks. The large building behind the water tank housed the Massachusetts Wharf Company. (Courtesy of the Society for the Preservation of New England Antiquities.)

This view reveals the interior of one of two Boston & Albany Railroad roundhouses located on lower Cambridge Street on the site of the present Allston Massachusetts Turnpike entrance.

The Boston & Albany Car Repair Shops, built in 1897, stood a few hundred feet west of the Allston Depot on the opposite side of the B&A tracks, bordering Lincoln Street. (Courtesy of the Society for the Preservation of New England Antiquities.)

This photograph offers an interior view of the Boston & Albany Railroad's Car Repair Shops. (Courtesy of the Society for the Preservation of New England Antiquities.)

Since the railroad crossed most Allston-Brighton streets at grade, accidents were frequent occurrences. The Everett Street Bridge, pictured here, was built in the early 1890s, seventy years after the construction of the railroad. (Courtesy of the Society for the Preservation of New England Antiquities.)

Prior to 1908, most of Allston-Brighton's river frontage was subject to tidal flooding. Extensive landfill operations were undertaken at the turn of the century. While engaged in one such project in November 1896, this crane collapsed into the marshes just west of the Faneuil Depot. (Courtesy of the Society for the Preservation of New England Antiquities.)

The whole Charles River Basin was systematically improved after 1908. Here we see Nonantum Road at Brooks Street under construction. To the right of the bridge stands the Faneuil Depot, partly obscured by a train. The building behind the depot is the Ensign Manufacturing Company on Parkman Street.

In 1900 the Boston & Albany Railroad was absorbed by the New York Central. This New York Central train is passing in front of the Faneuil Depot in the 1930s. The Watertown Arsenal is visible to the left. (Collection of Leon Onofri.)

This 1957 photograph shows the New York Central's "N.E. States Limited" speeding by the Allston Depot. The train is passing under the old Cambridge Street Bridge, which was replaced in 1962 by a larger span to accommodate the Massachusetts Turnpike Extension. (Collection of Kevin T. Farrell.)

A local commuter train stops at the site of the demolished Brighton Depot about 1958. (Collection of Leon Onofri.).

This 1910 photograph shows the old wooden North Beacon Street Bridge, one of several drawbridges that spanned the Charles River in Allston-Brighton.. The grounds of the Watertown Arsenal are on the right. A streetcar line then ran along North Beacon Street between Union Square and Watertown Square.

This view of the old North Beacon Street Bridge, dating from 1910, predates the construction of Nonantum Road. The houses in the background, lining Riverview Road, were razed when the Massachusetts Turnpike Extension was put through in 1962.

In 1912 the present concrete-and-steel North Beacon Street Bridge replaced the old wooden structure.

This 1899 photograph shows the wooden bleachers that originally occupied the Harvard Stadium site (extreme right). The Heaton Coal Company and Willard's Wharf then stood on the site of the Harvard Business School. The building to the right of the center of the photograph is Harvard's Carey Cage, demolished in 1996 to make way for a new athletic facility.

This view of the North Harvard Street Bridge, about 1910, shows the draw partially raised (left center). Harvard Stadium, visible behind the bridge, was constructed in 1903.

A new North Harvard Street Bridge was built in 1913. It was paid for by a gift of Harvard alumnus Larz Anderson in memory of his father, Civil War general Nicholas Longworth Anderson.

The upper end of Commonwealth Avenue, originally known as South Street, is being widened in this 1895 photograph. The construction crew stands on the site of the present Saint John's Seminary, opposite Evergreen Cemetery. The buildings in the distance line Chestnut Hill Avenue.

This 1899 photograph of Commonwealth Avenue near Warren Street shows the upper and lower roadways under construction. It was taken from the upper roadway looking across Allston towards Cambridge.

Streetcars operated on Commonwealth Avenue as early as the 1890s. This 1900 photograph shows a streetcar on the tracks between the upper and lower roadways north of Wallingford Road.

By the 1920s, Commonwealth Avenue in Allston had become Boston's Auto Mile. The most elaborate of the avenue's many showrooms was that established in 1910 by Alvan T. Fuller for Packard and Cadillac motor cars (right center) at the intersection of Commonwealth and Brighton Avenues. (Courtesy of the Society for the Preservation of New England Antiquities.)

This 1936 view of Washington Street at Commonwealth Avenue contains elements of the old and new—automobiles as well as a horse-drawn bakery wagon. The old house to the right, at 36 Washington Street, a vestige of old Brighton, contrasts sharply with such neighbors as the recently-constructed Washington Street Garage and the Baldwin Elementary School (center). (Collection of Kevin T. Farrell.)

The first official electric streetcar ride in Boston began here at the Allston Carbarn and Power Station, 43 Braintree Street, on December 31, 1888. Driven by Frank J. Sprague of the Sprague Electric Motor Company, the car traveled from Braintree Street to Park Square, Boston, and back. The most notable feature of the Allston facility was its towering, 100-foot chimney.

This 1938 photograph shows a streetcar on Wilton Street leaving the Allston Carbarn on Braintree Street. The bus garage building on the left still stands. (Collection of Mel Beaton.)

By 1889 electric streetcar service also extended into Oak Square. The massive Oak Square carbarn faced the north side of Washington Street just east of the square, and extended all the way back to Faneuil Street, on land now occupied by an MBTA parking lot and neighboring service station. Taken from the corner of Washington Street and Breck Avenue, this photograph dates from 1900. (Collection of Kevin T. Farrell.)

This view shows the front of the Oak Square carbarns on Washington Street about 1900. (Collection of Kevin T. Farrell.)

Here we see the interior of the Oak Square carbarns about 1900. The car barns were demolished in the mid-1920s. (Collection of Kevin T. Farrell.)

This 1938 photograph shows a streetcar reversing direction on the lot formerly occupied by the Oak Square carbarns. The open land at the extreme right was the site of the old Faneuil Mansion. Note should also be taken of the Crittenton-Hastings Hospital, dating from 1924, sitting atop Bigelow Hill. (Collection of Mel Beaton.)

Passengers board streetcars on lower Commonwealth Avenue near the Allston Street intersection about 1925. (Collection of Kevin T. Farrell.)

In the early years of this century, the Commonwealth Avenue streetcar line ran all the way to Newton's Norumbega Park, an amusement park that the street railway company established to attract riders. This 1910 view shows a streetcar taking on passengers at Commonwealth and Lake Streets (now the end of the line). (Collection of Kevin T. Farrell.)

A streetcar approaches the intersection of Brighton and Harvard Avenues in Allston in 1926. Notice the Allston Movie Theater to the right. In the absence of lights, a policeman directs traffic from a portable enclosure. (Collection of Kevin T. Farrell.)

This view of Brighton Avenue in Allston, dating from 1939, was taken near the intersection of Parkvale Avenue. By 1939, lights had been installed to handle the increasing traffic. (Collection of Kevin T. Farrell.)

Six

Institutional Life

The institutional life of Allston-Brighton attained great richness and variety in the late nineteenth and early twentieth centuries, a development well-documented photographically. Religious institutions were especially plentiful. Of particular note was the coming of a host of Roman Catholic institutions: five churches (Saint Columbkille's, Saint Anthony's, Our Lady of the Presentation, Saint Gabriel's, and Saint Ignatius); Saint John's Seminary for the training of priests; Saint Columbkille's and Saint Anthony's Schools; Mount Saint Joseph's Academy; Saint Gabriel's Monastery; the Cenacle and Franciscan Sisters of Africa Convents; and three hospitals, Saint Elizabeth's, Saint John of God, and the Kennedy Memorial (now the Franciscan Children's Hospital).

William Cardinal O'Connell contributed significantly to the expansion of these facilities. In 1918, theater owner Benjamin F. Keith bequeathed the Roman Catholic Archdiocese of Boston $2 million. The cardinal, who loved beautiful architecture, used the money to create a "Little Rome" on the hills of Brighton. One of the buildings he constructed with the Keith bequest was the archbishop's residence on Commonwealth Avenue, an Italian Renaissance palace dating from 1926.

Allston-Brighton's Protestant religious institutions also proliferated. The First Church (Unitarian) moved to a new headquarters on Chestnut Hill Avenue in 1895. The Congregationalists built two new houses of worship—in Allston and in Faneuil. Other Protestant denominations in Allston-Brighton included the Baptists, Universalists, Methodists, Episcopalians, and the Finnish Evangelical Lutherans.

By 1925, the community also contained a large Jewish population, concentrated in the vicinity of Commonwealth Avenue. A synagogue was established in 1933 in a converted private residence at 96 Chestnut Hill Avenue, at the corner of Wallingford Road. The burgeoning Jewish community soon outgrew this facility, however, and in 1951 built the massive Temple Bnai Moshe at 1845 Commonwealth Avenue.

Secular institutions also multiplied. The Ellen Gifford Animal Shelter was established on Undine Road before 1880. Many new schools were built, especially in the decade of the 1920s. The Florence Crittendon Home came to Bigelow Hill in 1924.

Of particular long-term significance was the location of three major universities on the periphery of Allston-Brighton: Harvard University began spreading across the Charles River into Allston as early as the 1890s, and continues building new facilities south of the river; Boston College moved from the South End to Chestnut Hill overlooking Brighton in 1909, and today the university's entire lower campus, including its athletic facilities and much of its student housing, lies within Allston-Brighton's boundaries; and, finally, Boston University, which opened its new Charles River campus in 1948, has been moving steadily westward towards Allston for years. The encroachment of these great institutions upon Allston-Brighton's residential neighborhoods will no doubt continue to be a matter of grave concern to the community in the years ahead.

In 1856, Allston-Brighton's first Catholic church, Saint Columba's, was established at 13-21 Bennett Street, just outside Brighton Center. By 1870 the congregation had grown to the point that a much larger building was required, and the present Saint Columbkille's Church was constructed at the northwest corner of Market and Arlington Streets. This photograph shows the church as it appeared during the 1880s, prior to the completion of its bell tower.

The first major Catholic institution to locate in Allston-Brighton was Saint John's Seminary. Work on Theology House, the seminary's Norman Chateau-style main building, began in 1881. Three years were required to complete the west wing, pictured here, which was constructed of darkish pudding stone quarried on the site. The chapel (right) was added in 1899.

This amazing panoramic view of the Chandler's Pond area, dating from about 1905, shows Lake and Kenrick Streets still largely undeveloped. Chandler's Pond was excavated for ice cutting in 1855. The house at the extreme right, which still stands at number 70 Lake Street, was the residence of ice dealer Malcolm Chandler. (Courtesy of the Society for the Preservation of New England Antiquities.)

In 1889 this large building was constructed at Saint John's Seminary for the Department of Philosophy. Philosophy House was destroyed by fire in 1936.

The second Roman Catholic institution to come to Allston-Brighton was Mount Saint Joseph's Academy, which was constructed on the former Henry B. Goodenough Estate on Cambridge Street in 1891. Pictured here is the original school and convent building, which was demolished in 1966.

As the number of Roman Catholics grew, additional churches were built in Allston-Brighton. The beautiful Romanesque Revival-style Saint Anthony's Church on Holton Street in North Allston, a work of noted ecclesiastical architect Franz Joseph Untersee, was built in 1904. This 1910 photograph also shows the church rectory. (Courtesy of the Society for the Preservation of New England Antiquities.)

The Passionist Missionary Society constructed Saint Gabriel's Monastery on the old David Nevins Estate in 1909. Considered the best surviving example of Spanish Mission-style architecture in Boston, it has been designated a City of Boston Architectural Landmark. (Courtesy of the Society for the Preservation of New England Antiquities.)

The Cenacle Convent came to Lake Street in 1910, at first occupying an old farmhouse that had belonged to the Benjamin Paine family. The north wing of the existing convent, pictured here, was constructed in 1912. The south wing was added in 1922. Noted architects Maginnis & Walsh designed the structure, which now houses the EF Language Institute.

Already a well-established institution, Saint Elizabeth's Hospital moved from the congested South End to this Spanish Mission-style structure in suburban Brighton in 1912. Its dramatic location on a hill overlooking Brighton Center made it a focal point of the neighborhood. The original building was demolished in 1983. This photograph was taken shortly after the completion of the 1912 structure. (Courtesy of the Society for the Preservation of New England Antiquities.)

The cardinal's residence on Commonwealth Avenue, on the grounds of Saint John's Seminary, built in 1926, has been described as "in the Roman style, [and] of stately and quiet dignity." William Cardinal O'Connell built this imposing residence as part of his plan to create a "Little Rome" on the hills of Brighton.

The Brighton Evangelical Congregational Church has occupied three buildings at 404 Washington Street in Brighton Center since its founding in 1827. Here we have the second of these buildings, a wooden Gothic Revival edifice, constructed in 1866 on the design of local architect George Fuller. This building was destroyed by fire in 1921.

Members of the Junior Christian Endeavor Society gather outside the Brighton Evangelical Congregational Church in 1900 .

A Universalist church was built at 341 Cambridge Street in 1861. When the congregation disbanded in 1887, the structure was acquired by Allston's Unitarians. In 1905 when the Unitarian congregation disbanded, the building was purchased by the Brighthelmstone Club, the community's leading women's club. The structure now houses the Allston Knights of Columbus Lodge.

Thomas W. Silloway, the second minister of the Universalist church, resigned his post in 1867 to pursue a highly-successful career in architecture. Silloway's works include the Vermont State House and some four hundred churches. The minister/architect resided in Union Square in Allston until his death in 1910.

In 1896 the Brighthelmstone Club was organized by the women of Allston-Brighton. Over the next quarter-century, this organization, an affiliate of the General Federation of Women's Clubs, established an impressive record. One of its early leaders was Harriet Baldwin, namesake of the Baldwin Elementary School. Another was Mrs. Florence Whitehill, mother of prominent historian Walter Muir Whitehill.

The Brighthelmstone Club

Announcements for November, 1919

Monday, November 3, 2.30 P.M.
Home Talent Day
Reception to New Members
Music   Tea

Tuesday, November 4, 8.00 P.M.
Mardi Gras. Under Auspices of the Art and Literature Committee. Tickets, 75 Cents

Thursday, November 6, 2.00 P.M.
Current Literature
Mrs. Marie A. Moore

Monday, November 17, 2.30 P.M.
Current Events Lecture
Mrs. Mabel A. Crawford
Music   Tea
Food Sale by Hospitality Committee

Thursday, November 20, 2.00 P.M.
Current Literature
Mrs. Marie A. Moore

The Art and Literature Committee announces a Class in Aesthetic Dancing on Fridays, at 10 A.M. Course of Ten Lessons, $7.50.

The Ways and Means Committee will have Christmas Cards for sale on each Club Day until Christmas.

MRS. WALTER M. WHITEHILL, *Pres't*
MRS. WILLIAM F. BURDETT, *Cor. Sec'y*
26 Glenville Avenue, Allston

The handsome Gothic Revival-style Allston Methodist Episcopal Church was built in 1876 at the southeast corner of Harvard Avenue and Farrington Street.

Methodist Church, Allston, Mass.

The magnificent Shingle-style Allston Congregational Church on Quint Avenue was built in 1890. Designed by Brighton architect Eugene Clark, it is considered to be the finest Shingle-style building in Allston-Brighton. The congregation was organized in 1886. Quint Avenue was named for the society's first minister, the Reverend Alonzo Hall Quint.

The Hill Memorial Baptist Church, built in 1903 at 279 North Harvard Street in Allston, was named in honor of an early benefactor, meat dealer Stephen Hill, whose residence is visible to the immediate right of the church.

Saint Luke's Chapel and Rectory were built in 1895 at Brighton Avenue and Saint Luke's Road in Allston. The present Saint Luke's Church was constructed in front of these structures in 1913, at which point the chapel became the congregation's parish house. (Courtesy of the Society for the Preservation of New England Antiquities.)

The Faneuil Congregational Church was founded in 1903 in a wooden building on Brooks Street. By 1913 the congregation needed a larger edifice. Here we see the May 1913 cornerstone-laying ceremony for the new building. The older structure is visible across Brooks Street (center). This building, now a private residence, served as the first home of the Faneuil branch of the Boston Public Library.

The 1913 Faneuil Congregational Church was constructed at the southwest corner of Brooks and Bigelow Streets.

Krokyn and Browne, Architects

When large numbers of Jews began moving into the Commonwealth Avenue area of Allston-Brighton, the nearest temple lay nearly three miles away. Congregation Bnai Moshe was formed in 1933. Its first permanent home, a converted house at 96 Chestnut Hill Avenue, served until 1951 when the present temple was built at 1845 Commonwealth Avenue.

Seven

Cultural Crossroads

From a predominately Yankee and Irish community in the mid-nineteenth century, through the addition of Jews, Italians, and other so-called "new immigrants" at the beginning of the twentieth century, to the more recent arrival of large numbers of Asians, Hispanics, Russian Jews, Afro-Americans, and Irish immigrants, Allston-Brighton has attained a cultural diversity second to no other community near Boston. That diversity is especially evident in the community's commercial centers, with their incredible array of ethnic restaurants, markets, and stores. Thus contemporary Allston-Brighton continues serving, as it has throughout much of its history, as a zone of emergence for recent immigrants, and a dynamic and stimulating urban cultural crossroads.

Allston-Brighton entered the twentieth century poised for rapid, high-quality suburban development, and by the 1920s many of its neighborhoods had achieved preferred suburb status. Unfortunately, a second wave of development in the post-World War II period depleted its supply of open land, subdivided its housing stock, clogged its roadways with traffic, and led to the demolition of many of its most valued historic landmarks. The 1950 to 1985 period was a time of especially intense and often shockingly indiscriminate over-development. While neighboring communities like Brookline, Newton, and Watertown were able to effectively regulate their development, Allston-Brighton lacked that opportunity by virtue of its political subordination to Boston.

The community has been more successful in recent years in coping with potentially damaging development proposals. It has learned to organize and to respond proactively. Few Boston neighborhoods can boast a larger population of watchdog associations. The oldest of these groups, the Allston Civic Association, was founded as early as 1963. The establishment of the Brighton-Allston Historical Society in 1968 reflected a growing concern to preserve the community's historic fabric. Other organizations have arisen to protect Allston-Brighton from damaging development: the Brighton-Allston Improvement Association, the Circle/Reservoir Community Association, and the Luck Neighborhood Association, among others. In many instances, ad hoc neighborhood groups emerged to oppose particular development threats. Notable also is a growing tendency for these groups to work together rather than in isolation. Contemporary Allston-Brighton has found its voice.

This new community spirit is manifested also in the vigor with which Allston-Brighton celebrated such important anniversaries as the national bicentennial in 1976 and the 350th anniversary of the founding of Boston in 1980. The new pridefulness is especially evident in the annual Allston-Brighton Parade, an event Allston-Brighton celebrates with pomp and enthusiasm every September since 1984.

On August 3, 1907, Allston-Brighton celebrated the 100th anniversary of the establishment of the Town of Brighton. The occasion was marked by a bonfire on "Dummy Field" on Everett Street in North Allston; by a one-hundred gun salute at the North Brighton Playground; and by a grand parade that ran up Cambridge Street into Brighton Center, culminating in literary and historical exercises at Wilson Park on Chestnut Hill Avenue. The featured speaker was town historian, J.P.C. Winship. This photograph of the festivities at Wilson Park shows, on the far

left, schoolchildren in red, white, and blue, forming a "living flag" on a platform adjacent to the Chestnut Hill Fire Station. The stand from which the day's speakers addressed the gathering lies at the extreme right. The large building in the background, the Holton Library, occupied the site of the present Brighton Branch Library on Academy Hill Road. Note the complete absence of automobiles from this 1907 scene.

This 1903 photograph of a third-grade class at the Harvard School in North Allston documents the presence of Afro-American families in that neighborhood. Long-time resident Wilfred J. Eagles noted of the Seattle Street/Windom Street/Amboy Street area of North Allston, "This is the only neighborhood I know of in the city of Boston where white and black people have lived together side by side, for generations, cooperatively and with harmony."

This *c.* 1910 view of children swimming on the shore of the polluted Charles River, near the present MDC skating rink, underscores the desperate need for recreational facilities for working class families. The high-rise structure in the background is the Perkins Institute for the Blind in Watertown. The Nonantum Road had not yet been constructed.

The Paul Revere Pottery was established in 1908 in Boston's North End by social reformer Helen Osborne Storrow to provide a safe and healthy work environment for young immigrant women. In 1915 it moved to 80 Nottinghill Road in Brighton, where it continued to operate until 1942. The English-style cottage structure has been converted into condominiums.

This structure at the northeast corner of Washington and Market Streets in Brighton Center, best known as the Rourke Building, is actually two separate structures: the Washington Building, dating from 1899 (the portion decorated with awnings) and the Imperial Hotel, built in 1909. Its prominent corner location and distinctive round corner tower make this Queen Anne-style building an important visual landmark. The photograph dates from about 1925.

BRIGHTON THEATRE

400 MARKET ST., BRIGHTON

PROGRAM—WEEK OF AUG. 6, 1916

SUNDAY, AUG. 6
Joe Jefferson and Zoe Beck in "The Beloved Liar"
Mary Fuller in "The Three Wishes"
Myrtle Gonzales and Fred Church in "Grouches and Smiles"

MONDAY AND TUESDAY, AUG. 7-8
Paul Panzer and Wm. Welch in "Behind the Secret Panel"
"Ignatz's Icy Injury," a spectacular comedy
Chapter Eight "Secrets of the Submarine"

WEDNESDAY AND THURSDAY, AUG. 9-10
Bluebird Feature—
Mary MacLaren in "Shoes" (A poor shopgirl story)
Billie Ritchie in "Bill's Narrow Escape"

THURSDAY, AUG. 10
Charles Chaplin in "The Vagabond"

FRIDAY AND SATURDAY, AUG. 11-12
"The Scorpion's Sting" (Underworld story)
Lee Hill and Marie Walcamp in "The Money Lenders"
Alice Howell in "How Stars are Made"
Animated Weekly

MATINEE AT 2.30--Adults 10c., Children 5c.
EVENING AT 7.45--Admission 10c.
Program changed four times a week

The Brighton Theater, also known as The Barn, was located at 400 Market Street on the site of the present municipal parking lot. Brighton Center's first motion picture theater, it was built about 1915, in the silent movie era. It went out of existence shortly after the nearby Egyptian Theater opened in 1929.

With the introduction of talking movies in 1929, theater audiences expanded to such an extent that much larger facilities were required. Brighton's Center's Egyptian Theater, which opened in 1929 at 326 Washington Street, was one of the handsomest of these new movie palaces.

The lobby of the Egyptian Theater is
shown here as it appeared about 1940.

The sumptuous Egyptian Theater, with its exotic decor, could accommodate an audience of
1,700. Although the theater closed its doors in the late 1950s and was subsequently demolished,
a portion of its foyer was incorporated into the Brighton Elks Hall, which now occupies the site.

Here we see the interior of Dan's Market at 1 North Beacon Street in Union Square in 1929. The owner, Dan Cantoni (right) resided on nearby Armington Street. The young man on the left is longtime Allston resident Garnett Long, then age ten.

This photograph of student cadets marching in front of Brighton High School on Warren Street in 1931 shows the site of the Franciscan Children's Hospital (formerly the Kennedy Memorial Hospital). A stone quarry called McMurtry's Ledge had existed at this site for many years.

This 1938 view of Brighton Center looking east shows a commercial apartment building that once stood at the corner of Washington and Cambridge Streets, on what is now the Saint Elizabeth's Hospital grounds. Built in the 1890s at a time when the hill was slated for residential development, it was taken down by the hospital in the 1940s. (Collection of Mel Beaton.)

In this 1940 view of Brighton Center looking west from Nevins Hill, one sees in the left foreground two structures that have since disappeared: the commercial apartment complex on Saint Elizabeth's grounds (a rear view), and to its left, at the corner of Winship and Washington Streets, the old West End Street Railway carbarn. The carbarn dated from the late 1880s.

ALBERT PICKENS

134 KENRICK STREET
BRIGHTON, MASS.

ANNUAL SPRING SALE

OF 100 HEAD OF

Show & Saddle Horses & Hunters

INCLUDING THE

Entire Show Stable of Miss Jane Bancroft

COHASSET, MASS.

Monday Evening, April 17
Tuesday Evening, April 18

BEGINNING AT 8 P. M.

COL. EARL B. THOMPSON
AUCTIONEER

TEL. ALG. 9732

In the late 1920s, a large ice house at the western end of Chandler's Pond was converted into a horse stable. In 1933 the stable was owned and operated by Albert Pickens. Later it became the property of the Keith family. The Keith Stable burned in a spectacular fire in the early 1950s. Here we have the cover of a 1933 Pickens Stable horse auction catalog.

This 1938 photograph shows a streetcar passing by Gray's Market when it stood at its original site on Washington Street between Breck Avenue and Nonantum Street. The store to the right is Moore's Drug Store. (Collection of Mel Beaton.)

This 1940 view shows a streetcar on Cambridge Street in Allston just north of the Hano Street intersection. (Collection of Mel Beaton.)

By 1943 the Oak Square carbarns had been demolished. Little remained to reflect the square's former importance as a transportation terminus. In the foreground is Smith's Open Air Market. This photograph also shows the old configuration of the Oak Square Common, which has since been extensively altered to facilitate the smooth flow of traffic. (Courtesy of the Society for the Preservation of New England Antiquities.)

This view of Oak Square looking south towards Langley Road and Breck Avenue shows how extensively Nonantum Hill had been developed by 1943. Notice how the commercial block on the south side of Washington Street then extended all the way to the Breck Avenue intersection. The right-hand section was later demolished to make way for a service station. (Courtesy of the Society for the Preservation of New England Antiquities.)

This 1945 photograph of Union Square shows a Mobil gas station on the site where the handsome Brighton Avenue Baptist Church stood prior to its destruction by fire in 1929. Today the Union Square Fire Station occupies this highly-visible location. Major alterations in Union Square's traffic patterns necessitated the relocation of the Hanoville Associates World War I memorial, which appears at the center of this photograph. (Courtesy of the Society for the Preservation of New England Antiquities.)

Passenger service to the Allston Depot was discontinued in the 1950s. This photograph of Dick Keefe, the last Allston Depot ticket agent, was taken on September 10, 1948, by local railroad buff Jack Leonard. (Courtesy of Jack Leonard.)

North Allston's Smith's Field, now the McKinney Playground, is about to celebrate July Fourth with a traditional bonfire. The photograph dates from the early 1950s. The houses on the extreme right formed part of the Barry's Corner neighborhood, which was demolished by the BRA in the late 1960s. (Courtesy of Jack Leonard.)

This wintertime 1950 view of Chandler's Pond was taken from the grounds of the Chestnut Hill Country Club. It shows the area now occupied by Towne Estates and the Chandler Pond Apartments prior to development, which was then a popular site for sledding. (Courtesy of Jack Leonard.)

The stucco commercial building at the center of this 1950 photograph of Market Street near the Market Street Burying Ground no longer stands. The Federal-style brick structure to the left, which once belonged to the Sparhawk family, and dates from the very early 1800s, has been "modernized." (Courtesy of Jack Leonard.)

Allston-Brighton celebrates the national bicentennial on July 4, 1976, with a grand parade. Flag-waving celebrants line Washington Street in Brighton Center.

Public officials, including longtime State Representative John Melia (second from the left), review the Allston-Brighton Parade in Brighton Center in September 1984, with the new Saint Elizabeth's Hospital building under construction in the background.

Children view the first Allston-Brighton Parade in September 1984.

This 1985 photograph of children standing in front of the Oak Square Methodist Church reflects the rich ethnic and cultural diversity of contemporary Allston-Brighton. To the left stands the Reverend Steven Griffith, and to the right, the Reverend Souen Sorth (a Cambodian minister).